Turtles

John F. Waters

ILLUSTRATED BY BILL BARSS

Follett Publishing Company Chicago

ISBN 0-695-40176-9 Titan binding
ISBN 0 695-80176-7 Trade binding
Library of Congress Catalog Card Number 78-118957
Second printing

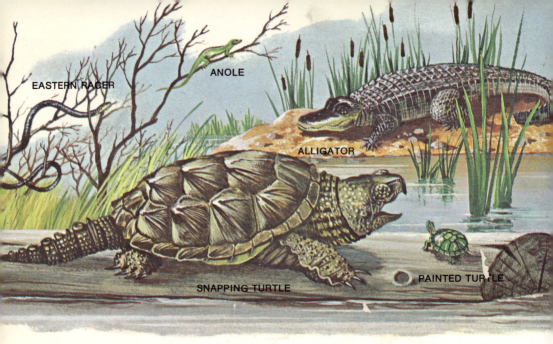

EASTERN RACER

ANOLE

ALLIGATOR

SNAPPING TURTLE

PAINTED TURTLE

Reptiles have backbones. Their bodies are covered with scales or shells. There are over 6,000 different kinds of reptiles on the earth today.

Turtles are reptiles that have shells. Other well-known reptiles are snakes, lizards, crocodiles, and alligators. Turtles are smarter than most reptiles, but not as smart as mammals, such as dogs or cats.

Like other reptiles, they do not have much heat inside their bodies. They tend to be as cool or as warm as things around them.

4

TURTLES

A Follett Beginning SCIENCE Book

READING CONSULTANT
Jeanne S. Brouillette
Former Curriculum Coordinator
Evanston Elementary Schools
Evanston, Illinois

TECHNICAL CONSULTANT
Clifford H. Pope
Former Curator of Amphibians and Reptiles
Field Museum of Natural History
Chicago, Illinois

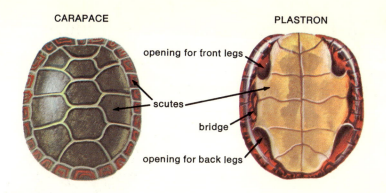

CARAPACE

PLASTRON

opening for front legs

scutes

bridge

opening for back legs

The carapace and plastron are covered with horny plates called scutes. The shape, color, and number of scutes vary from one kind of turtle to another. The place where the two shells come together is called a bridge. To record a turtle's size, scientists usually measure the length of its carapace.

The shell on a turtle's back is called the carapace. A turtle's backbone is just underneath the carapace and attached to it. The shell that protects its belly is called the plastron. The carapace and plastron are usually fastened together at the sides. As a turtle grows, its shell grows, too.

Each kind of turtle has its own kind of shell. Some shells are smooth; others are rough with bumps or ridges or points. Some are flat; others are more rounded. Some shells are even soft.

Turtles that spend most of their life in water usually have flatter shells. Those that live on land tend to have higher shells.

GOPHER TORTOISE
Size: 6-11 inches
Range: Southwest United States

ATLANTIC GREEN TURTLE
Size: 2-4 feet
Range: warmer parts of Atlantic Ocean

A green turtle swims by paddling with his front feet. His back feet are used for turning left and right in the water. The gopher tortoise walks upon the claws of his front feet, and the back feet are flat against the ground.

All turtles have four legs and a tail, but some have very different feet. The feet of sea turtles are flippers that can also be used for walking. Desert turtles have short, stumpy legs that look like small elephant feet.

Turtles have long necks that can curl into an S and fit inside the shell. They can also pull their head and legs inside the shell. This keeps them from being eaten by other animals.

A turtle's head is snakelike. The eyes do not have two eyelids, as ours do. The mouth has a hard, horny beak with cutting edges instead of teeth. Turtles will spit out things they do not like to eat. They have a wide tongue, a sense of taste, and a good sense of smell. They also have a good sense of touch.

The alligator snapping turtle eats fish and small water animals. It catches food by hiding in muddy waters with its mouth open and wiggling a wormlike object hooked to its tongue.

The red ears on this turtle often change to yellow as it gets older. Like all turtles, the red-eared turtle has three eyelids. There is a thick upper lid, a thin lower lid, and a thin lid that moves sideways across the eye.

ALLIGATOR SNAPPING TURTLE
Size: 26 inches
Range: rivers of south
United States and Mississippi
River area

RED-EARED TURTLE
Size: 5-7 inches
Range: freshwaters of
midwest and southwest
United States

7

CHICKEN TURTLE
Size: 10 inches
Range: waters of south
and southeast United States

When the chicken turtle is upset, it will make a hissing sound.

Turtles do not hear very well. They do notice or "feel" movements of the earth or water. Most turtles have no voice, but a few can make barks or grunts. Some make sounds when they breathe or rub their jaws together.

SPOTTED TURTLE
Size: 3-5 inches
Range: northeast and
east United States

This shy turtle makes a good pet. It likes to swim in small ponds and swamps.

Water turtles can hold their breath under water for about two or three hours. They have large lungs and use oxygen slowly when under water. Some of them can take oxygen from the water as well as from the air. They suck water in and then pump it out. This helps them get oxygen from the water the way fish gills do. This allows them to stay under water for a longer period.

EASTERN MUD TURTLE
Size: 3-5 inches
Range: southwest, midwest,
and Gulf Coast of United States

The Eastern mud turtle will bury itself in mud or old wood before winter comes.

Turtles that live where winters are cold bury themselves before winter comes. Then they go to sleep. Their heartbeat is very slow. They do not breathe because they do not need much oxygen. They do not have to eat because there is food stored inside their bodies. In the spring, when the earth warms up, they crawl out of the mud or burrow.

Turtles that live in the ocean or hot desert do not sleep during the winter.

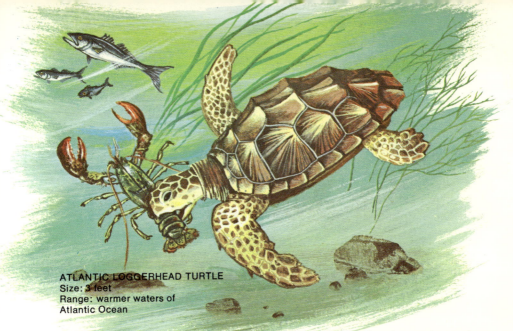

ATLANTIC LOGGERHEAD TURTLE
Size: 3 feet
Range: warmer waters of
Atlantic Ocean

The loggerhead turtle has strong jaws that can break the hard coverings of shellfish.

What turtles eat depends on where they live. Sea turtles eat fish, jellyfish, clams, and turtle grass.

Land turtles eat insects, slugs, snails, and earthworms. Others eat leaves, berries, and various plant parts. Some have claws on their front feet for tearing up their food. Most turtles eat regularly when they can, but some are able to go a year without food. They drink water when they can find it.

Even if she lives in water, a mother turtle lays her eggs on land. Eggs are usually laid in the spring.

The mother turtle may have to clear the area with her front feet. Then she digs a hole with her rear feet. Where she digs depends on where she lives. So she may dig in sand, mud, or dead leaves on the forest floor. She may lay only one or two eggs or as many as 200. This depends on what kind of turtle she is. After the eggs are laid, she covers the nest using her rear feet.

Female turtles never look at the eggs they lay.

BLANDING'S TURTLE
Size: 7-8 inches
Range: southeast Canada
to midwest United States

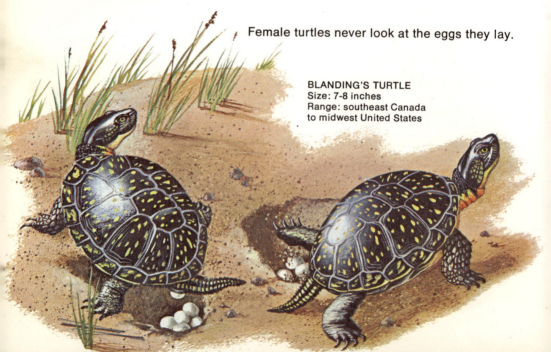

Large turtles lay eggs about the size and shape of golf balls. The eggshells feel like leather and are white or cream colored.

The sun's heat helps the baby turtles to grow inside the eggs. This takes about three months. The babies usually break out of their eggs in early fall. In places where winters are very cold, turtle eggs hatch the next spring.

Unhatched reptiles and birds receive their food supply from the egg yolk and water from the egg white. The turtle egg has a larger egg yolk than the chicken or robin eggs.

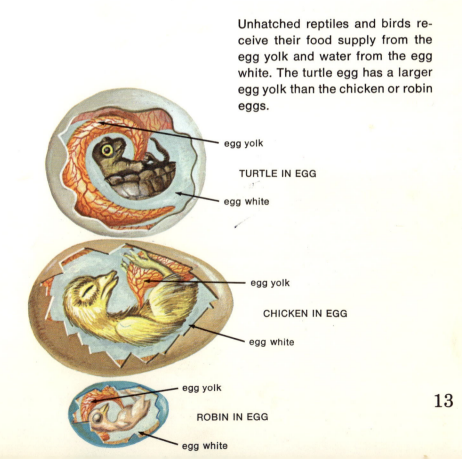

egg yolk

TURTLE IN EGG

egg white

egg yolk

CHICKEN IN EGG

egg white

egg yolk

ROBIN IN EGG

egg white

Neither father nor mother turtles care for the eggs, so the baby turtles are always on their own. When baby turtles hatch, they are about two inches long and look something like their parents. At first, their little bodies have soft shells, so they are defenseless. They hide most of the time. When their shells harden, they are better protected. Some are almost full grown in four or five years. But they continue to grow a very little for the rest of their lives. Some kinds live for 50 years and some for 100 years and longer.

The young spotted turtle is about one inch long when it hatches. It has one yellow spot on each scute of its carapace. Spots will appear on its tail and legs as it gets older.

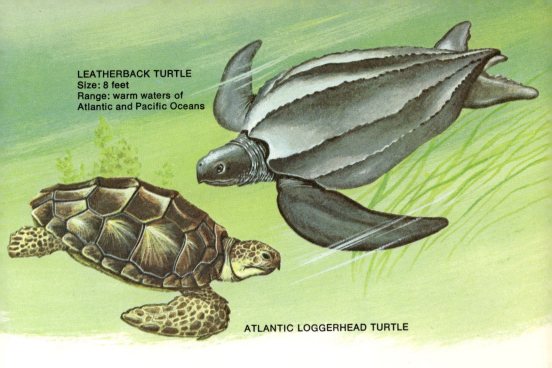

LEATHERBACK TURTLE
Size: 8 feet
Range: warm waters of
Atlantic and Pacific Oceans

ATLANTIC LOGGERHEAD TURTLE

A leatherback turtle does not have a rough, hard shell like other sea turtles. Its shell is smooth.

Both of these sea turtles are able to sleep while floating on top of the water.

There are over 200 kinds of turtles in the world. The largest kind, the leatherback, lives in the sea. Some leatherbacks weigh as much as 1,500 pounds or more. Loggerhead and green turtles also live in the sea and weigh between 500 and 1,000 pounds.

ATLANTIC GREEN TURTLE

A green turtle looks something like a loggerhead turtle, but the green turtle has a larger head.

The green turtle is found in the Atlantic and Pacific Oceans. It is a large sea turtle with flippers and can swim for thousands of miles. When ready to lay eggs, the green turtle returns to the same beach where it was hatched. The eggs and meat of this turtle are considered choice food by many people. A delicious soup is made from calipee found inside its bottom shell.

The soft-shelled turtle has such a long neck
it can get air without leaving the water.
Nostrils are located at the tip of its long snout.
It does not have to poke its head completely
out of the water to get air.

Soft-shelled turtles have a brown shell
that is a thick, soft skin. Their shells are never
hard. They are found in ponds and rivers over
most parts of the United States.

SOFT-SHELLED TURTLE
Size: 18 inches
Range: North America,
Africa, Asia, and Malaysia

DIAMONDBACK TERRAPIN
Size: 8 inches
Range: east United States

The meat from the diamondback terrapin is good to eat.

Some water turtles are called terrapins. The diamondback terrapin lives in the salt marshes along our eastern coast. It was named after the pattern of plates on its upper shell. The design of each plate reminded people of a cluster of diamonds. Its shell may vary from light brown to black. It has webbed feet instead of flippers. Its head and legs are spotted. Sometimes the diamondback swims in the open sea, but it usually lives in salt marshes and tidal rivers.

AFRICAN SOFT-SHELLED TORTOISE
Size: 1-3 feet
Range: East Africa

The soft-shelled tortoise lives in the water during the rainy season.

Certain land turtles, especially those that live in deserts, are called tortoises. In Africa there is a small soft-shelled tortoise that lives among rocks. It has a thin, flexible shell. To escape danger, it can squeeze into rock crevices. This tortoise takes in air and swells up like a balloon, so that it becomes fastened safely in the crevice.

DESERT TORTOISE
Size: 8-12 inches
Range: southwest United
States

Both the desert tortoise and the gopher tortoise dig burrows, but the gopher tortoise digs much deeper into the ground.

The desert tortoise digs a burrow that is often shared with other animals. It needs to live in such places to escape the hot sun and sometimes the cold nights. It has large, stumpy rear legs. It eats cactus, grass, and some insects. Indians ate the meat of the tortoise and used the shells for cups and bowls. It is found in the far southwestern part of the United States.

GALAPAGOS TORTOISE

The Galapagos tortoise is so friendly that children can ride on it. This large reptile must stay on land because it cannot swim.

The giant tortoise is found only on the Galapagos Islands. These islands are on the equator about 600 miles west of South America. Their name is Spanish and means tortoise. The giant tortoise looks like an upside-down bathtub. It has legs thicker than a man's legs. After hatching, it is only three inches long, but grows to be over five feet in length. It is the largest of all land turtles. Some of them may live to be over 200 years old.

EASTERN

PAINTED TURTLES
Size: 5½-7 inches
Range: east, west, and
south United States

SOUTHERN

WESTERN

These turtles eat water plants, small animals, and insects.

The painted turtles are perhaps the most colorful. Their upper shell is an olive or dark brown color with yellow and red marks. Their legs are also brightened with yellow and red streaks. Their lower shell is yellow and sometimes has a dark figure on it. Their feet are webbed for swimming. Sometimes they like to leave their pond or stream and walk on land. They also like to crawl up on logs or stones to sun themselves.

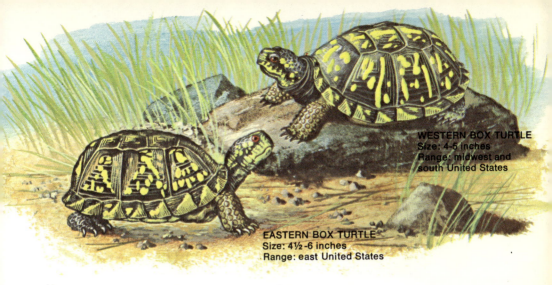

WESTERN BOX TURTLE
Size: 4-5 inches
Range: midwest and
south United States

EASTERN BOX TURTLE
Size: 4½-6 inches
Range: east United States

Box turtles are only found in North America.

Box turtles have a plastron with a hinged flap in front. After a box turtle pulls its neck inside, the flap closes tightly like the lid of a box.

Box turtles live in prairies and open woodland. On hot days they like to sit in water to cool off. They eat many things, such as insects, snails, earthworms, fruits, and sometimes mushrooms. They make good pets and need only a backyard or a box of dirt for digging and a shallow pan of water for bathing. They are fond of raw hamburger.

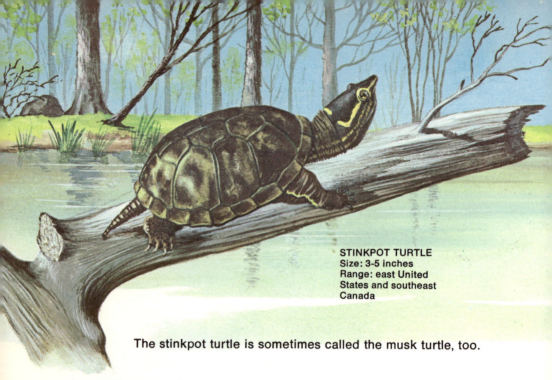

STINKPOT TURTLE
Size: 3-5 inches
Range: east United
States and southeast
Canada

The stinkpot turtle is sometimes called the musk turtle, too.

The stinkpot turtle was named for a good reason. It gives off an offensive odor when disturbed. It has a nasty temper and bites.

It lives in the water, mostly in larger ponds and lakes. It likes to climb out on the slender trunks of trees that lean over the water. A stinkpot turtle sleeps the winter away in the mud under a few inches of water. It eats crayfish, fish, insects, snails, and some plants.

SNAPPING TURTLE
Size: 13 inches
Range: southeast Canada,
east United States, and
east Mexico

The snapping turtle spends much time in the water, but is not a good swim-mer. It is not friendly and would not make a good pet.

The common snapping turtle deserves its name. From the moment it is hatched, the snapping turtle strikes out with its strong jaws at anything that moves. It is an ugly-looking turtle. Its shell is dark brown and its head is very large. It can catch small fish and tadpoles for food.

WOOD TURTLE
Size: 6 inches
Range: New England
and midwest United States

This turtle likes to eat fruits and vegetables.

The wood turtle likes to wander through woods, meadows, and farmlands. Sometimes it is seen crossing a road or a highway. Its shell is brown and very rough. Its neck and feet are orange.

It is one of the smartest turtles and also one of the best to have for a pet. It cannot stand very hot sun for long periods of time. If it did not bury itself deep in the bottom mud of a lake or pond before winter arrived, it would die.

Early whalers caught tortoises on the Galapagos Islands for food. Today in some parts of the world there are laws to protect turtles and stop man from killing them.

People have eaten the meat and eggs of certain turtles for centuries. Early whaling ships took giant tortoises aboard for fresh meat; some of them would live upside down for almost a year in the ship's hold before they were eaten. The green turtle and its eggs are still much sought as food. Meat from soft-shelled turtles was once covered with corn meal and fried. The diamondback terrapin has been called the most famous of all turtles as a choice food.

Always handle your turtle carefully or it may be hurt. A turtle should be picked up by holding on to the back part of its carapace. Then you can carefully hold it in the palm of your hand. It is important to wash your hands after handling your pet turtle.

Maybe you would like to keep a turtle for a pet. See if you can buy a small one at a pet shop or variety store. If its shell has been painted, scrape or peel the paint off carefully. The paint is not good for the little turtle's health.

The large turtles you may find near a pond or in the woods require larger pens and tanks.

MUHLENBERG TURTLE

This turtle is a good one to keep as a pet because it is small and friendly.

Most pet turtles need to be kept warm, usually at temperatures between 75° to 80° F. They should be kept in a small glass or plastic tank. There should be a place where the turtle can crawl out of the water and bask in sunlight.

The turtle tank should be cleaned about once a week. Everything should be removed. The sides and bottom of the tank should be washed with soap and water. Then the tank should be rinsed thoroughly.

The best diet for small pet turtles is a mixture of meat, vegetables, and fruit.

They can be fed carrots, lettuce, tomatoes, apples, bananas, watercress, watermelon, oranges, and peaches. For meat, you can use bits of fish, chopped beef, liver, shrimp, lobster, or even canned dog food.

Feed your turtle about three times a week. If it is very young, it can be fed daily. The food should be left in the tank for no more than two hours. Then remove any uneaten food so it will not spoil the turtle's water.

If your turtle loses its appetite, his new home may be too cool or too warm.

If properly cared for, your turtle will prove to be a fun and interesting pet.

Words Younger Children May Need Help With
(Numbers refer to page on which the word first appears)

4 anole
5 carapace
  plastron
  scutes
6 tortoise
8 jaws
10 burrow
11 loggerhead turtle

12 Blanding's turtle
15 leatherback turtle
16 calipee
17 Malaysia
18 tidal rivers
   diamondback
     terrapin
19 flexible

   crevices
21 Galapagos Islands
23 mushrooms
24 musk turtle
25 tadpoles
29 Muhlenberg turtle
30 watercress
   watermelon

THINGS YOU CAN DO

Visit an aquarium or a museum of natural history. Most aquariums have sea turtles in their saltwater tanks. Notice the smooth swimming strokes the sea turtle makes with its front flippers. Also, look at the sharp beak and the scales on its head.

There may be a large turtle shell on display at the museum. Notice how the backbone is attached to the carapace.

Keep a turtle as a pet. You can buy a turtle in a pet store, or you may want to catch a turtle in the woods or near the water. Make sure the turtle is a friendly kind before you handle it. It is important to take a turtle from an area where the water is clean and unpolluted, too.

Most turtles need to be kept warm, usually at temperatures between 75°F. to 85°F. Water turtles should be kept in a tank made of glass or plastic which is deep enough for the turtle to be covered completely with water. Some turtles need to swallow their food when their heads are underneath the surface of the water.

There should be an area where the turtle can crawl when it isn't in the water. This is important for basking turtles. They need at least eight hours of bright light or sunlight per day, but not direct sunlight that is very hot.

The tank needs to be cleaned once a week. Everything should be removed from the tank. The sides and bottom are then washed with soap and water. Finally, the tank is thoroughly rinsed.

Turtles can eat carrots, lettuce, kale, watercress, tomatoes, peaches, oranges, bananas, cantelope, apples, and watermelon. Those kinds that eat meat will like bits of lobster, shrimp, liver, beef heart, chopped beef, or canned dog food. The best diet for most turtles is a mixture of meat, vegetables, and fruit.

Adult turtles can be fed three times per week, but younger ones can be fed daily. Food should be left in the tank for about two hours, and then all uneaten bits should be removed. This will help keep the water clean.

Turtles may become ill if not cared for properly. Their most common illness is "soft shell." This is caused by lack of calcium. Foods that are high in calcium need to be included in their diet, too. If a turtle doesn't appear hungry and is difficult to feed, the temperature in the tank might be too low. It is important to watch the temperature level closely. Finally, if the shell of the turtle is painted, scrape or peel off the paint. Paint will impair growth and could eventually kill the turtle if it isn't removed.